EMBROIDERY GARDEN

ARTFUL DESIGNS
INSPIRED BY NATURE

yanase rei

SCHIFFER
CRAFT

4880 Lower Valley Road • Atglen, PA 19310

Preface

The embroidery garden I would like to create resembles a very small world. It's a garden with lots of plants that will surely excite anyone who gazes upon it.

Here you will find not only beautiful, wonderful, gorgeous plants, but also poisonous flowers and weeds, and even things that are fun like goofy horses, pigs, and birds.

The garden will look different in the morning, afternoon, and evening. It's fun to imagine and embroider plants and flowers that will bloom at different times of the day.

It's always okay to change the image you are working on, even if you are in the middle of creating the overall pattern. Also, there is nothing wrong with tight, clean stitching. However, it is also fine if your stitches aren't perfectly uniform.

If you patiently continue to embroider, eventually you will improve your stitching skills. And one day, you will find that you can no longer produce those not-so-skilled stitches you made when you just started embroidering, even if you try. I sometimes miss those beginner stitches, all raw and powerful. In the end, regardless of skill level, whatever you achieve with your current embroidering skills will be precious.

After working on several embroidery projects, you'll enjoy seeing improvement in your work by spotting not-so-skilled stitches in earlier projects and comparing them to the improved stitches in your more recent projects.

I mean for the embroidered flowers in this book to be used as a reference, but my greatest wish is for you to invest time in creating your very own embroidery gardens with personalized flowers.

yanase rei

Contents

Delicate and Light

The botanical motif embroidery in this
section uses a single strand of No. 25
embroidery floss. Since a single strand
produces less volume, detailed depictions of
the motifs are used in order to create a bit
of density. The result is a delicate and light
form of embroidery that resembles lace
needlework. If you intend to produce a three-
dimensional effect, use two strands to make
French knot stitches and three strands for
bullion stitch roses. Rather than individual
motifs, it is the beauty of the overall
composition and lines that is the hallmark of
these embroidery pieces.

1 Black background fabric amplifies the rich beauty of the colorful flowers. The ambience is a celebration of the night forest.
Embroidery pattern ▸ **page 66**

The piece from page 8 can be mounted in a frame. Feel free to embroider all the way out to the edge of the image area or just leave the background fabric around the embroidery as shown in the picture. Frame: 30.5 × 23 cm / 12" × 9"

Sample Project

2 The color combination used here is like being under a pale light. The piece appears fragile, but in reality, the plants are thriving and growing tall. Pattern ▸ page 68

8 Embroider a flowing pattern, sort of like it is inside a belt. The background fabric is the same, but different patterns and floss colors can heavily influence the look of the fabric itself. Embroidery pattern ▸ **page 70**

4 These bow ties, with their delicate embroidery, can easily be worn by anyone. Attaching is simple; just use the brooch pin on the backside. How to ▶ **page 100**

14   **5** The pattern consists of leaf motifs only. The top half of the pattern exclusively uses white embroidery floss. The use of colored embroidery floss on the lower half of the pattern adds cuteness to the work. The color influences the texture of the embroidery work.   Embroidery pattern ▶ **page 72**

6 Unique and beautiful plants, with their gentle color combinations, sometimes give you an unsettling feeling when gazing upon them. This work has the perfect balance of both conditions.   Embroidery pattern ▸ **page 74**

7 Thinking of an exotic and distant country. Any part of this pattern can easily be removed to make a unique embroidery pattern.
Embroidery pattern ▸ page 76

৪ The patterns on pages 20 and 21 show leaf motifs that have been taken from works presented on pages 8 through 19. Embroidery pattern ▸ **page 79**

You can make small embroidery pieces that include a single plant motif or combine a few motifs together.

Embroidery pattern ▸ page 79

What Do You Like?

My embroidery, as you have already seen, isn't a carbon copy of real plants. I love plants and have been around them since I was a child, so I have seen a lot of them. That being said, I prefer an embroidering style that is "an expression of my favorite plants," rather than "carefully observing and making precise copies of plants." I don't feel like I absolutely have to re-create my favorite plants; I can just embroider what I like.

When I closely examine unknown plants and fallen or dead leaves on the ground, sometimes I find their shapes really interesting. Even when examining familiar plants, if I look at them from unusual angles or if they change colors, I find something that I like in them. If you have a stock of such favorites, they may inspire you to create fernlike or some kind of herb-like embroidery motifs. It doesn't matter if their colors and shapes are different from the original, or if they become abstract. Just like paintings, I believe it is acceptable to combine different elements to make interesting embroidery pattern components. Also, I should mention that I find great inspiration in museum exhibits and books. Even if they aren't directly related to embroidery, the lively expressions and brilliant writings, along with the overwhelming worldview that a novel or museum exhibit presents, greatly stimulate me. I realize that not all of my favorites need to be sources of inspiration, but the accumulation of exploring every avenue of thought I come across helps me create embroidery.

When I create plant motif embroidery, I always imagine something cute on somebody else, but not on myself. The someone can be a friend or a random person I saw on the street who left an impression on me. It's fun to embroider while imagining what would look good on that person. What do they like? What is their favorite activity? I encourage you to give shape to such thoughts through embroidery.

Hostas. The characteristics of balance between veins, colors along leaf edges, color density, and wandering curves are all interesting to me.

Fatsi. Leaves splay out from the top of the strangely long and thin stems. This imbalance is very attractive. Shapes created in nature have interesting details and a sense of self-assertion.

I tend to focus on the flowers when thinking of violets. But, the cute way they grow freely is my favorite part.

The view of a thistle from above. Buds can be seen in the center of jagged leaves, giving it a rustling vitality.

My favorite books. They are in different genres, such as art and food, but all of them are wonderful.
The book *Hana no teshigoto* (The Handiwork of Flowers) by Keita Maruyama was given to me by my teacher. It is so beautiful that I can't help but sigh and look at it over and over again.

I am attracted to wisteria and azalea by the density of the small flowers and colors. Even though the flowers are small, I feel that their concentration creates a sense of presence and magnificence.

Moss on an azalea. There is an interesting balance between peeling and chipping. The color is slightly different in various parts, and the moss covers the branch in flower-like shapes. Moss is mysterious.

10 Bookmarks embroidered with patterns presented on pages 8 and 18. Every part of the pattern possesses a certain presence.   How to ▶ page 102

The Grace and Beauty of Black

Black is a color that I often choose because of its ease of use. However, while easy to use, it is also a strong color. This section suggests how to use black to produce a sophisticated look. The embroidery is done on black, beige, or brown base fabric with black No. 25 embroidery floss. Without the appeal of colorful embroidery, this combination can produce extremely striking and beautiful scenes. The only drawback is that it is difficult to see the floss when working on the stitches!

11 This piece has a cute feel because of the round flowers. Black looks especially beautiful with the luster and volume of satin stitches.
Embroidery pattern ▸ page 80

12 This embroidery pattern exclusively gathers together leaf motifs. If the embroidery piece on page 26 expresses a night garden, this one is a deep forest at night. Embroidery pattern ▸ page 81

13 Beads glow within this narrow strip-like embroidery. The combination of black and somber gold brings about a lustrous and luxurious feel. Embroidery pattern ▸ **page 82**

14 The embroidery from the facing page is tailored to be a hatband. I used beige as the backing material to match the color of the beads so they would peek out. Adjust the length according to the hat size.   How to ▸ page 104

15 The beige-colored background fabric softens the black embroidery. This piece describes jagged and thorny-looking plants in a silhouette-like style. Embroidery pattern ▸ page 83

16 This black case uses the embroidery pattern from page 32. The beige fabric liner encases the black fabric like a picture frame. Use this lovely folded case for your pens, pencils, or even cutlery. How to ▸ page 106

If black embroidery floss is densely stitched, it will be difficult to see the individual stitches. In this case, it is better to present motifs in a silhouette-like style, use linier stitches, or create distinctive designs.   Embroidery pattern ▸ **page 85**

Color Preference

Color is important. I believe that you can use any color you desire. A pink sky, bright-blue leaves, black flowers – anything is possible. However, it is important to unify the tones and images so that elements won't become disjointed within the piece. After choosing a background fabric, decide what kind of image you want to embroider. Do you want it to be cool or a little gentle? Even if the envisioned image is the same, the colors selected will vary by individual. It's so nice that embroidery floss is available in a variety of colors, but that also means it is troublesome to decide on just one.

To match red fabric, select a well-balanced color palette that consists of similar colors – ranging from red through purple. Add yellow and blue as accent colors. In my embroidery, yellow and blue are never the main colors. You might think that green would be a good color to accentuate red, but green is for foliage, so it is usually more interesting to deviate from the standard color scheme.

This color palette has an elegant image that can be used for anything. This example combines off-white fabric with gentle neutral-colored embroidery floss. For this kind of gentle and elegant combination, I recommend using a dense and detailed motif or a dynamic motif. These colors look good around the face, so they can be used as a turban or headdress.

This example was derived from the image of flowers blooming at night. Black fabric highlights the colors well and makes them look even more beautiful. Use the two red embroidery flosses on the right for the flowers, and use the rest for the leaves. Even though the leaves have the same shape, their impression changes when stitched with different-colored embroidery floss.

The Progression of Embroidery Work

Sometimes people ask me, "Where do you start stitching?" Most of the time, I embroider without transferring the pattern onto fabric, and I make stitches to fill spaces on the fabric and embroider in multiples. But yes, where do I actually start? For this piece, I did give it some thought and looked for a good starting and ending point. That way I wouldn't get lost in the middle of the project.

At the end, fill spaces with small plants.

I often place a flower motif, the main focus, at the bottom center of the pattern. Begin working on the main flower motif and then move left to right. Next, work your way up above the main flower motif, before moving left to right again. As shown in the photo above, I began stitching at the bottom of the pattern and moved upward. I stitched the leaves and stems so they would follow the contours of the adjacent flower's leaves and stems. At the end, I stitched some small plants to fill the spaces between the motifs. In most cases, my embroidery work progresses from bottom to top. Occasionally, I am at a loss at to what to embroider. However, in the end it is a chance to explore new ideas, so it's actually a pleasant experience.

19 This brooch has a flower motif chosen from the piece presented on page 10. Bordered by cords, this brooch feels somewhat like a coat of arms.   How to ▸ **page 110**

Dynamism and Presence

This section introduces works that use two strands of No. 25 embroidery floss. Stitches with two strands give the plant motifs a definite shape and add presence to the overall pattern. Also, combining floss colors is much more enjoyable than stitching with a single strand.

20 Pink creates a calm and serene ambience. This color combination is exquisite. The green foliage uses three different-colored pieces of floss, while the brown foliage uses two different-colored pieces. Embroidery pattern ▸ **page 86**

21 The embroidery piece on the facing page is tailored to be a hairband. It is like wearing the plants themselves!　How to ▸ **page 108**

22 Elegant is the perfect word for this piece. The nearly symmetrical composition of the plants also gives a sophisticated impression. It's interesting to compare this piece with that presented on page 10 to see the differences between single-strand and double-strand works. Embroidery pattern ▸ page 88

23 Beads represent dazzling rain. The dense bullion stitch creates delicate rose petal layers.   Embroidery pattern ▸ page 90

24 The red fabric easily draws one's attention, so rather than filling the surface with embroidery, we can just use beads to embellish half of the surface. This makes the pouch both casual and practical.   How to ▸ **page 107**

25 This group of quirky plants gives the sense of arid land where grass scents are all afloat. If you create this pattern using different-colored floss, it will drastically change the feel of the piece.　Embroidery pattern ▸ page 92

This is the embroidery work from page 46 in a frame. The texture of the frame matches well with the embroidery. Frame size: 30.5 × 23 cm / 12" × 9"
Sample Project

26 Three types of leaf motif embroidery pattern. They all repeat simple shapes. As in the pattern shown on top, it is fun to combine a few colors.   Embroidery pattern ▸ page 94

27 Animal motifs are cuter when capturing similarly shaped animals' features. Make the animal motifs fantastical, as if they were illustrations in a picture book.   Embroidery pattern ▶ page 96

28 The facing page shows a motif taken from the embroidery work presented from pages 40 through 51.
Embroidery pattern ▸ **page 98**

29 Any part of this embroidery pattern, stitched with two strands of embroidery floss, can easily be taken out to make an individual pattern. Which is to say, it can be used for single-motif embroidery.   Embroidery pattern ▸ **page 99**

My Creations

From time to time, I have the opportunity to team up and collaborate on a project. Even though there are some rules, such as the theme and size of the project, I have been fortunate enough, in general, to be able to embroider as I please.

Though it's not embroidery, I have made some jewelry for theatrical plays before. Of course, every play tells a story and, based on the design drawings I received from the costume designer, I created jewelry with materials, colors, and shapes that would leave a lasting impression. There are many things I learned from working on these theater projects; primary among them was the fact that you need to "make what isn't there."

Of course, I experienced many failures throughout the process of learning. Even so, the joy of working with a team and achieving a goal is something that one can never experience alone.

This is an embroidery work I made, at the request of a client, with the theme of "Being inside a bag." If it was an ordinary bag, I could have used fabric, but the bag was meant for the dancer inside to express herself. So, I figured it would be better if the dancer's body was visible. I decided to use a transparent plastic bag, but the problem with plastic is that it tears easily. After trying various materials, such as garbage bags, I was able to embroider using one strand of black No. 25 embroidery floss and the thinnest needle possible. Using this I carefully inserted long stitches. This project expresses the idea of "A human being born from flowers."

Dancer: Mayumu Minagawa
Photographer: Saki Matsumura
Hair & Makeup: Kaori Miyazaki

Left: Trial and error. Deciding on floss color and types of vinyl sheeting.
Right: Work in progress with black embroidery floss.

I also made casual jewelry. The necklace on the left (see photo) uses colored black resin pearls at both ends. The middle is colored cork clay, which gives the necklace texture. The necklace at the right (photo) is made of coral and colored resin pearls. The earrings are a mix of various materials. The materials can be found at arts and crafts stores, and I try to use items that catch my eye. It can be anything that draws your attention or just something you find interesting. Don't use each material as is; instead, try to change the color or add some personal touches.

Sometimes you can't tell what will happen when you make changes to material. It might be misleading to say that we will always turn a mistake into a success, but even if something ugly is the end result, it can still be made into something interesting. The important thing is to find balance and at least try to make improvements.

I try to make jewelry that has impact but isn't too flashy. Or to make things that aren't too cute when worn by mature women.

How about embroidering on a ready-made blouse? I casually stitched white leaves along the chest and scattered them along the hem at the back.
Sample Project

Materials

1. Various Fabrics You can use plain or patterned fabric. Choose any fabric you like. However, be aware that it is difficult to embroider on coarse woven fabric.

2. Fusible Interfacing Fuse on backside of embroidered fabric when making a bag, etc.

3. No. 25 Embroidery Floss This book uses DMC embroidery floss.

4. Beads This book mainly uses Delica Beads (Japanese seed beads). Feel free to use your preferred beads. Sequins can be used as well.

5. Satin Ribbon The bookmark uses a fine satin ribbon.

6. Silk Cord Use silk cord for drawstring bags, brooch borders, etc.

Embroider while freely enjoying colors and patterns. Use your preferred fabric and embroidery floss.

Tools

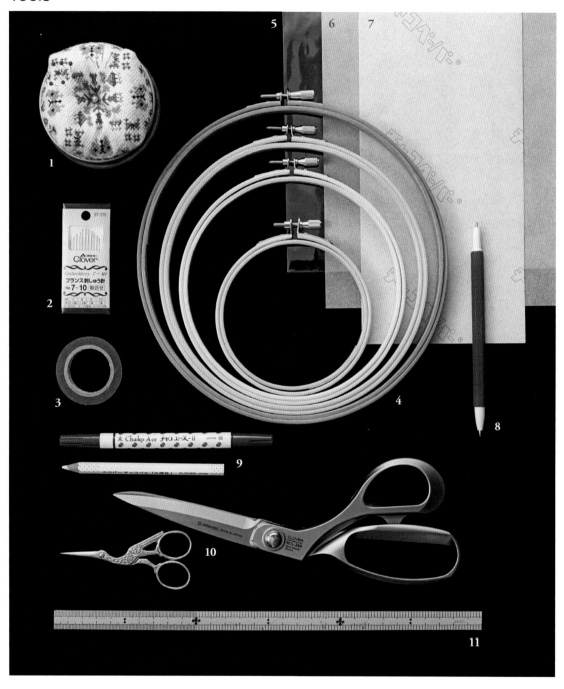

1. Pincushion

2. Chenille Needle Use size 8, regardless of the number of strands of embroidery floss you use.

3. Masking Tape Convenient for securing copied patterns when transferring.

4. Embroidery Hoop A variety of sizes are available. The most commonly used size is 15 cm / 6", but everyone has their own preferred size. Begin with 12 cm / 4" or 15 cm / 6".

5~7. Cellophane (OPP bag), Tracing Paper, Chalk-Based Transfer Paper Used to transfer patterns onto fabric.

8. Stylus Use to trace patterns when transferring onto fabric.

9. Marking Pencil or Pen For drawing pattern directly on fabric, or marking fabric for cutting/sewing.

10. Scissors Prepare both embroidery scissors and fabric shears. Use sharp embroidery scissors with a pointed tip.

11. Ruler A short, narrow ruler is convenient.

The tools noted above are just the basics. Feel free to choose any other tools that you are comfortable using.

Stitching Methods
These are my own stitching methods for the plants in this book.

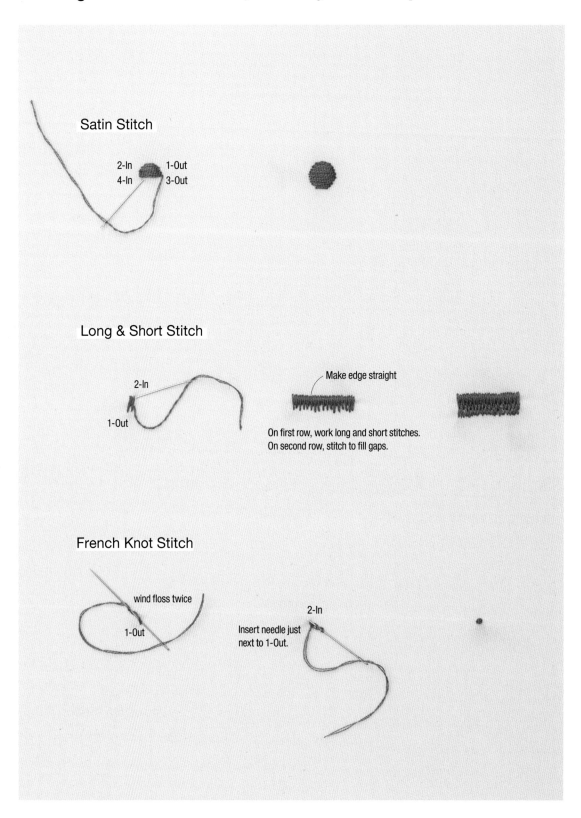

Satin Stitch

2-In   1-Out
4-In   3-Out

Long & Short Stitch

2-In

1-Out

Make edge straight

On first row, work long and short stitches.
On second row, stitch to fill gaps.

French Knot Stitch

wind floss twice

1-Out

2-In

Insert needle just
next to 1-Out.

Lazy Daisy Stitch + Straight Stitch

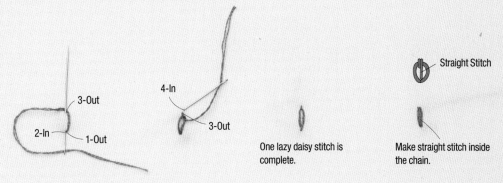

3-Out

4-In

3-Out

2-In — 1-Out

Straight Stitch

One lazy daisy stitch is complete.

Make straight stitch inside the chain.

Outline Stitch – two strands of floss

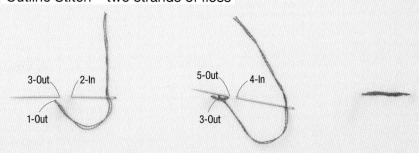

3-Out   2-In

1-Out

5-Out   4-In

3-Out

Outline Stitch – one strand of floss

* Can be stitched using two strands of floss.

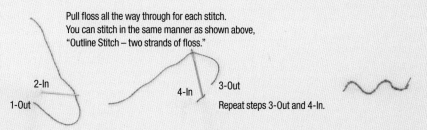

Pull floss all the way through for each stitch.
You can stitch in the same manner as shown above,
"Outline Stitch – two strands of floss."

2-In

1-Out

4-In   3-Out

Repeat steps 3-Out and 4-In.

Stitch That Gradually Increases in Width

outline stitch

Align with outline stitch – stitch in the same manner as the satin stitch – but increase stitch length little by little as you go.

Bullion Stitch Rose

* Bullion stitch roses presented in this book use three strands of floss.

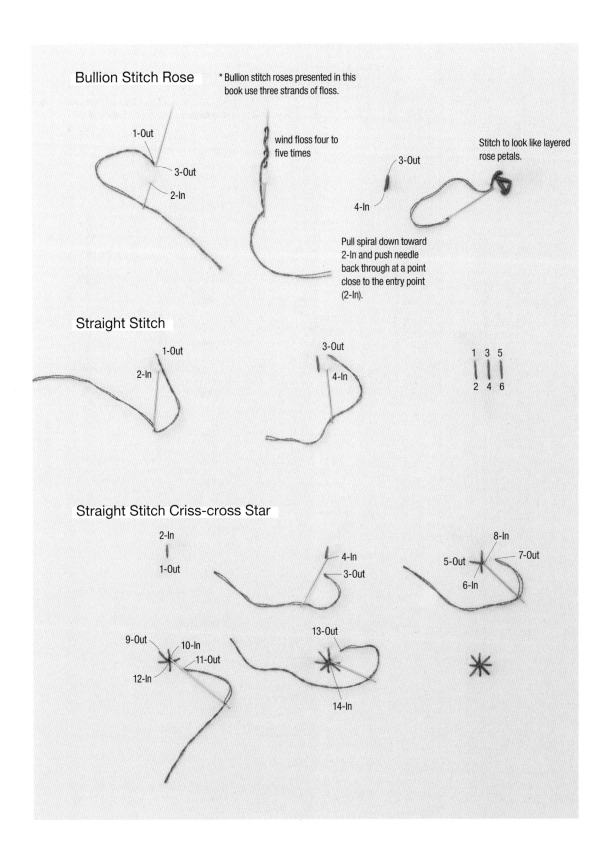

1-Out
3-Out
2-In

wind floss four to five times

3-Out
4-In

Pull spiral down toward 2-In and push needle back through at a point close to the entry point (2-In).

Stitch to look like layered rose petals.

Straight Stitch

1-Out
2-In

3-Out
4-In

1 3 5
2 4 6

Straight Stitch Criss-cross Star

2-In
1-Out

4-In
3-Out

8-In
5-Out
7-Out
6-In

9-Out
10-In
11-Out
12-In

13-Out
14-In

I randomly layer straight stitches in order to produce a certain nuanced look on flowers and leaves. I often combine outline stitches, straight stitches, and satin stitches for leaves.

Transferring Patterns

Photocopy or trace the pattern onto tracing paper. Secure the copied pattern on the right side of fabric with pins. Insert chalk-based transfer paper between the fabric and pattern. Lay cellophane over the pattern (secure with tape) and trace the pattern with a stylus. When using pale colored fabric, lay fabric on top of pattern and trace to transfer.

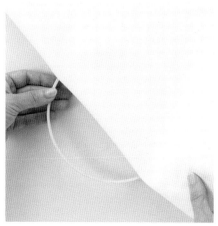

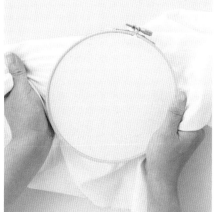

Securing Fabric in Embroidery Hoop

Unscrew and separate inner and outer hoops. Lay fabric over inner hoop and place outer hoop over that, while keeping the fabric flat. Tighten screw. Pull fabric edges to tighten the fabric in the hoop a bit more. Always tighten fabric to your preferred tautness before stitching.

30 The white brooch (top) uses the same pattern as the brooch on page 38. The red brooch (bottom) uses the flower pattern on page 52. How To ▸ **page 110**

Instructions

- Units of measurement are primarily cm. Though this book provides measurements in inches, it should be noted that they are approximate conversions only.

- Figure dimensions and patterns do not include seam allowances unless otherwise indicated. Add 1 cm / ⅜" seam allowance. Cut fabric without adding a seam allowance where labeled "No Seam Allowance."

- Fabric sizes given on figures have some room for adjustments. Use fabric that is thick enough to be stable in an embroidery hoop.

- The letters "st" in diagrams are an abbreviation for "stitch." The abbreviation RS stands for Right Side, and WS stands for Wrong Side of fabric.

- Completed work dimensions may differ from measurements given on diagrams.

- This book gives color numbers for DMC embroidery floss.

- Feel free to substitute your preferred materials. Combine your own choices of embroidery flosses and colors to create the desired effect.

- Patterns without enlargement scales are full sized. Where enlargement scales are specified, make enlarged photocopies accordingly.

Stitches: Use one strand of floss. Use outline stitch for contours and elongated shapes. Use straight stitch or satin stitch to fill areas and short lines.

Color #

Pale Flowers 80% Scale Pattern. Enlarge the 80% scale pattern to 125% to produce the full-size pattern.

Stitches: Use one strand of floss. Use outline stitch for contours and elongated shapes. Use straight stitch, French knot stitch, or satin stitch to fill areas and for short lines.

Outline st · Straight st · Outline st · Straight st · French Knot st, 2 strands · Outline st · Satin st (coarse stitches) · Straight st · Long lines: Outline st · Outline st · Straight st · Outline st · Outline st · Straight st

Color #

Stitches and Color #: Use one strand of floss. Use outline stitch for contours and elongated shapes. Use straight stitch or satin stitch to fill areas and for short lines.

Top — Bottom

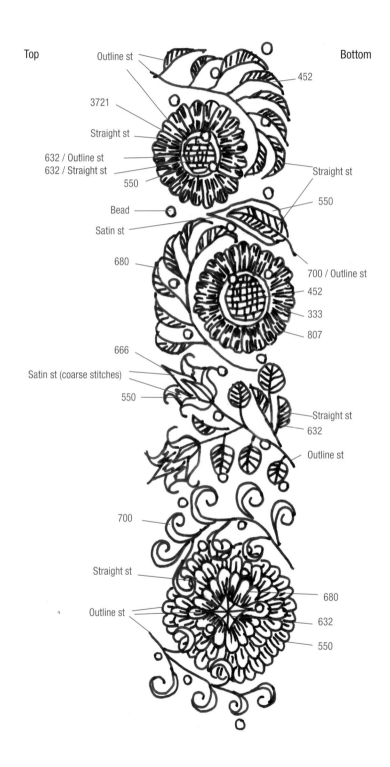

Outline st
452
3721
Straight st
632 / Outline st
632 / Straight st
550
Straight st
550
Bead
Satin st
680
700 / Outline st
452
333
807
666
Satin st (coarse stitches)
550
Straight st
632
Outline st
700
Straight st
680
Outline st
632
550

Stitches and Color #: Use one strand of floss. Use outline stitch for contours and elongated shapes. Use straight stitch to fill areas and for short lines.

Use 452 for all stitches.

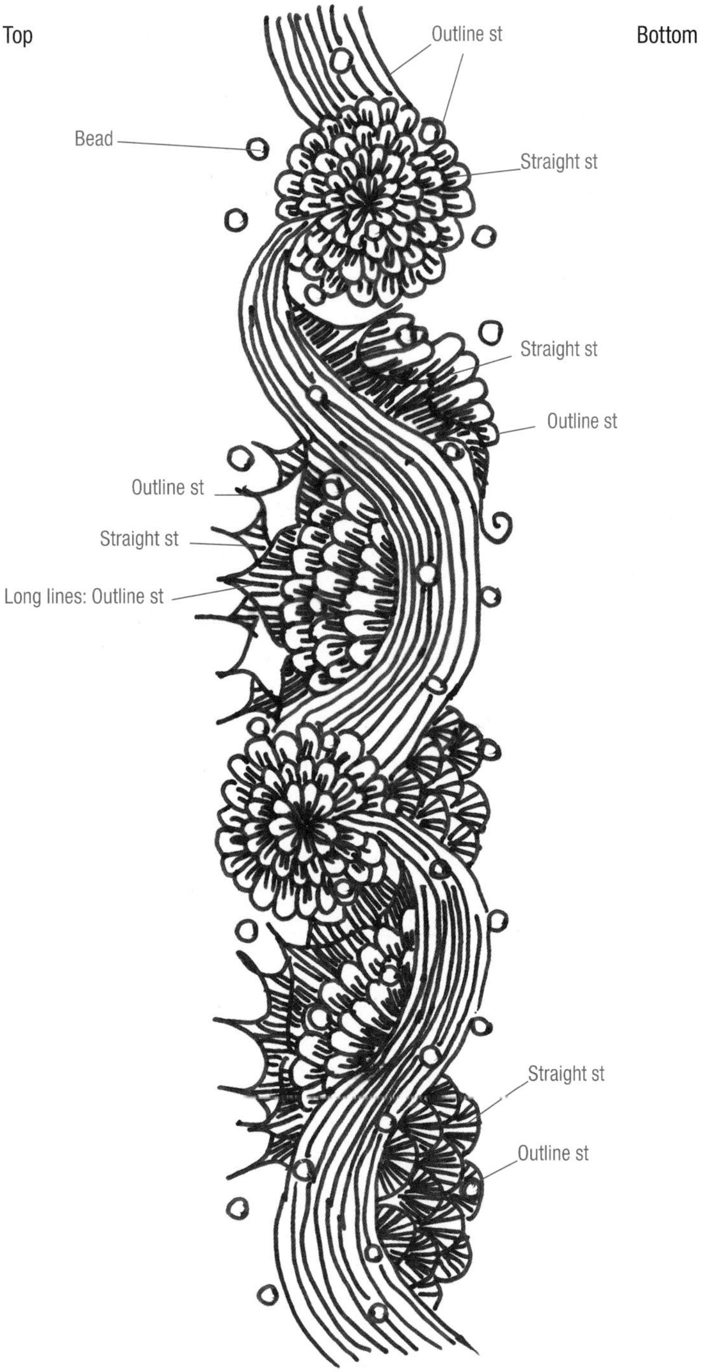

Top

Bottom

Outline st

Bead

Straight st

Straight st

Outline st

Outline st

Straight st

Long lines: Outline st

Straight st

Outline st

White and Colorful Leaves 80% Scale Pattern. Enlarge the 80% scale pattern to 125% to produce the full-size pattern.

Stitches: Use one strand of floss. Use outline stitch for contours and elongated shapes. Use straight stitch or satin stitch to fill areas and for short lines.

Straight st

Outline st

Straight st Criss-cross Star

Lazy Daisy st + Straight st, 2 strands

Straight st

Satin st

Outline st

Straight st

Outline st

Straight st

Outline st

Outline st

Outline st

Straight st

Straight st

Outline st

Straight st

Outline st

Straight st

Color #

B5200

3832

826

915

3777

319

352

680

152

471

210

152

352

924

702

948

702

924

829

210

3863

632

319

White and Pink Flowers 80% Scale Pattern. Enlarge the 80% scale pattern to 125% to produce the full-size pattern.

Stitches: Use one strand of floss. Use outline stitch for contours and elongated shapes. Use straight stitch to fill
areas and for short lines.

Color #

3778

3778

BLANC

BLANC

3778

BLANC

80% Scale Pattern. Enlarge the 80% scale pattern to 125% to produce the full-size pattern.

Stitches: Use one strand of floss. Use outline stitch for contours and elongated shapes. Use straight stitch and satin stitch to fill areas and for short lines.

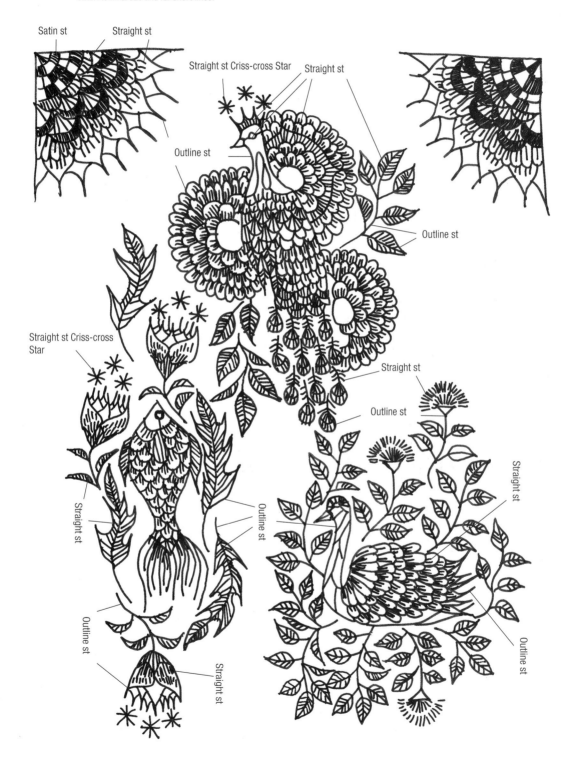

Satin st

Straight st

Straight st Criss-cross Star

Straight st

Outline st

Outline st

Straight st Criss-cross Star

Straight st

Outline st

Straight st

Outline st

Outline st

Outline st

Straight st

Straight st

Outline st

Color #

Stitches and Color #: Use one strand of floss. Use outline stitch for contours and elongated shapes. Use straight stitch or satin stitch to fill areas and for short lines.

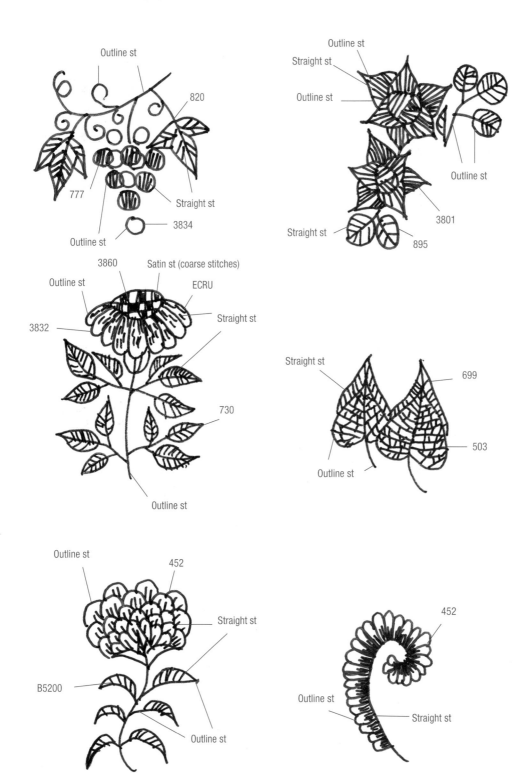

Stitches and Color #: Use one strand of floss. Use outline stitch for contours and elongated shapes. Use straight stitch to fill areas and for short lines.

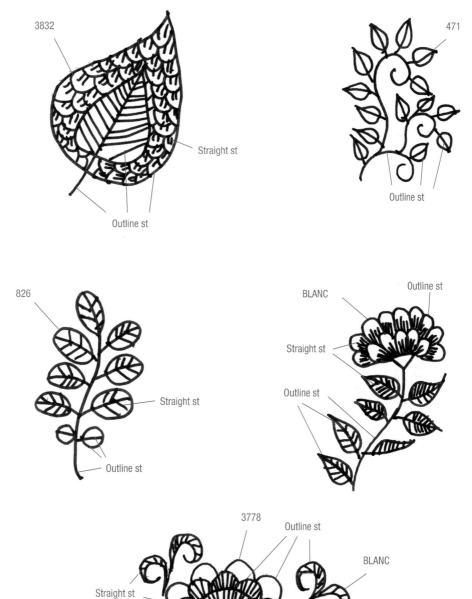

3832

Straight st

Outline st

471

Outline st

826

Straight st

Outline st

BLANC

Outline st

Straight st

Outline st

3778

Outline st

BLANC

Straight st

80% Scale Pattern. Enlarge the 80% scale pattern to 125% to produce the full-size pattern.

Stitches and Color #: Use two strands of floss. Use outline stitch for contours and elongated shapes. Use straight stitch and satin stitch to fill areas and for short lines.

Use 310 for all stitches.

French Knot st

Outline st

French Knot st

Satin st

Straight st

Outline st

Lazy Daisy st + Straight st
Fill in gaps with Straight st

French Knot st

Outline st

French Knot st

Satin st

Outline st

Satin st

Satin st

Outline st

Satin st

Outline st

Stitches and Color #: Use two strands of floss. Use outline stitch for contours and elongated shapes. Use straight stitch and satin stitch to fill areas and for short lines.

Use 310 for all stitches.

Straight st

Straight st, 1 strand
Outline st

Straight st

Outline st

Satin st

Satin st

Straight st

Outline st

Straight st

Satin st

Satin st

Satin st

Straight st Criss-cross Star

Lazy Daisy st + Straight st

Outline st

Satin st

Satin st

80% Scale Pattern. Enlarge the 80% scale pattern to 125% to produce the full-size pattern.

Stitches and Color #: Use two strands of floss. Use outline stitch for contours and elongated shapes. Use satin stitch to fill areas.

Use 310 for all stitches.

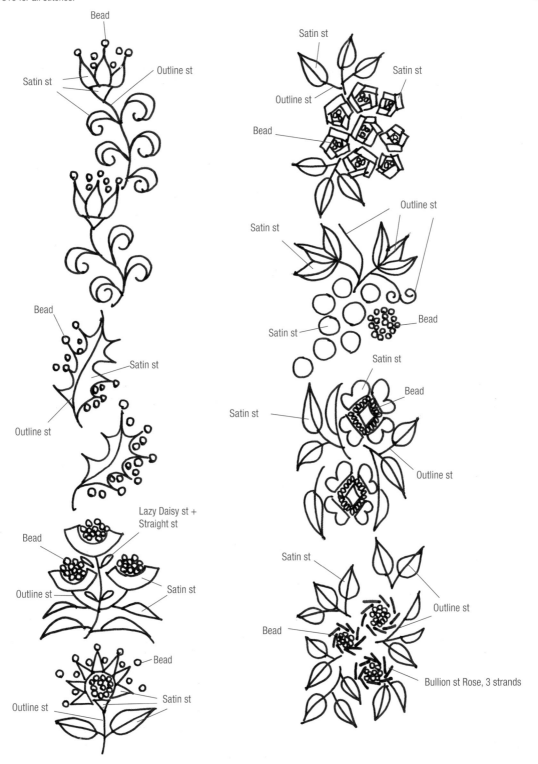

80% Scale Pattern. Enlarge the 80% scale pattern to 125% to produce the full-size pattern.

Stitches and Color #: Use two strands of floss. Use outline stitch for contours and elongated shapes. Use satin stitch to fill areas.

Use 310 for all stitches.

Straight st, 1 strand sticking out and short

Satin st

Satin st

French Knot st

Outline st

Lazy Daisy st + Straight st

Straight st over Satin st, use 1 strand of floss, offset each stitch.

Satin st

Satin st

Satin st

Outline st

Satin st

Satin st

Outline st

French Knot st

Satin st

Outline st

French Knot st

Satin st

Lazy Daisy st + Straight st

French Knot st

Satin st

Outline st

Stitches and Color #: Use two strands of floss. Use outline stitch for contours and elongated shapes. Use straight stitch and satin stitch to fill areas and for short lines.

Use 310 for all stitches.

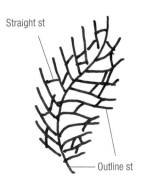

Straight st

Outline st

Satin st

Outline st

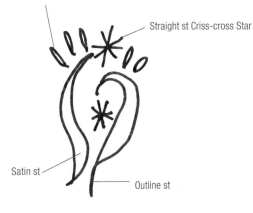

Lazy Daisy st + Straight st

Straight st Criss-cross Star

Satin st

Outline st

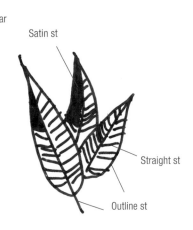

Satin st

Straight st

Outline st

Lazy Daisy st + Straight st
Fill in gaps with Straight st

Outline st

Satin st

French Knot st

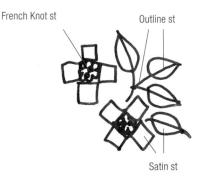

French Knot st

Outline st

Satin st

Stitches and Color #: Use two strands of floss. Use outline stitch for contours and elongated shapes. Use satin stitch to fill areas.

Use 310 for all stitches.

French Knot st

Straight st, 1 strand
Short, sticking out

Satin st

Satin st

Outline st

Satin st

Satin st

Outline st

Lazy Daisy st + Straight st

Outline st

French Knot st

Satin st

Straight st over Satin st, use 1 strand of floss, offset each stitch.

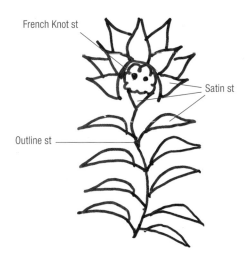

French Knot st

Satin st

Outline st

80% Scale Pattern. Enlarge the 80% scale pattern to 125% to produce the full-size pattern.

Stitches: Use two strands of floss. Use outline stitch for contours and elongated shapes. Use satin stitch to fill areas.

Color #

Stitches: Use two strands of floss. Use outline stitch for contours and elongated shapes. Use satin stitch to fill areas.

French Knot st

Bullion st Rose, 3 strands

French Knot st

Outline st

French Knot st

Satin st

Outline st

Satin st

Outline st

Satin st

Satin st   French Knot st   Satin st   Straight st   Lazy Daisy st + Straight st

Color #

Stitches: Use two strands of floss. Use outline stitch for contours and elongated shapes. Use satin stitch to fill areas.

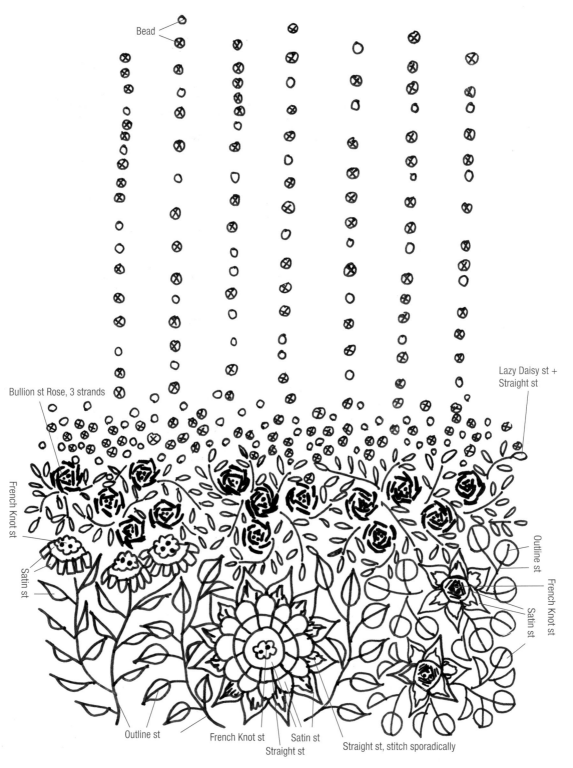

Bead

Lazy Daisy st + Straight st

Bullion st Rose, 3 strands

French Knot st

Satin st

Outline st

French Knot st

Satin st

Outline st · French Knot st · Satin st · Straight st · Straight st, stitch sporadically

Full-Size Pattern

Color #

Top   Bottom

25 Yellow Leaves and Flowers 80% Scale Pattern. Enlarge the 80% scale pattern to 125% to produce the full-size pattern.

Stitches: Use two strands of floss. Use outline stitch for contours and elongated shapes. Use satin stitch to fill areas.

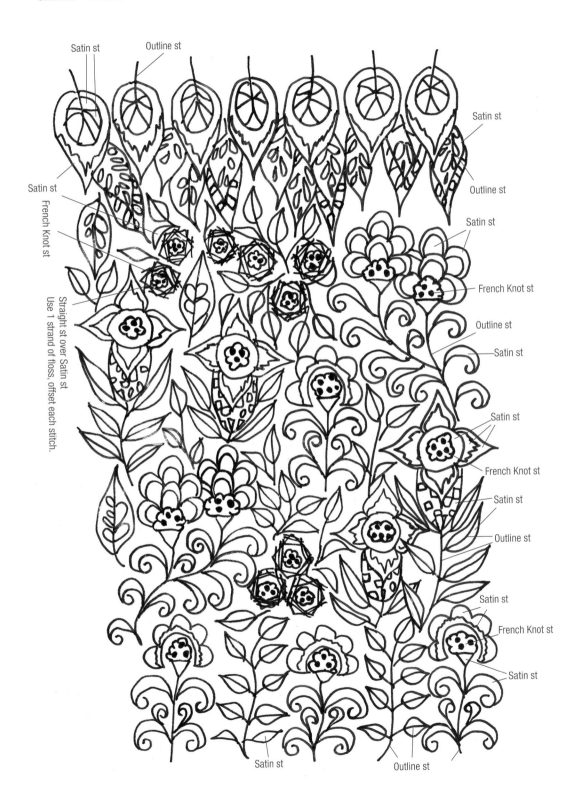

Color #

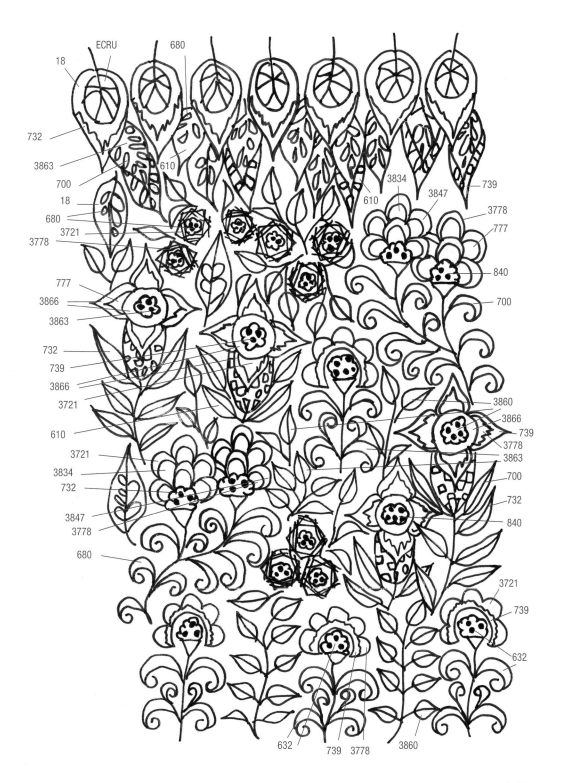

Stitches and Color #: Use two strands of floss. Use outline stitch for contours and elongated shapes. Use satin stitch to fill areas.

Top

Bottom

35

Satin st

400

Outline st

Satin st

610

Outline st

3847

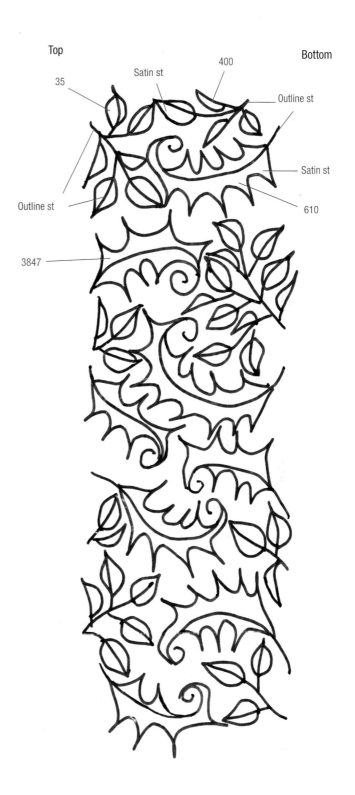

Stitches :   Use two strands of floss. Use outline stitch for contours and elongated shapes. Use long & short stitch and satin stitch
to fill areas.

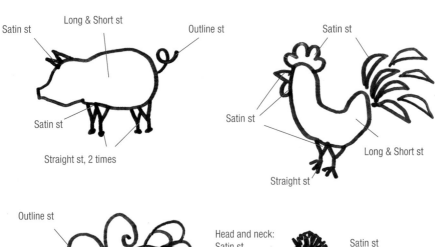

Satin st   Long & Short st   Outline st

Satin st

Straight st, 2 times

Satin st

Satin st

Long & Short st

Straight st

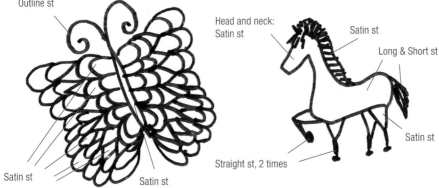

Outline st

Head and neck:
Satin st

Satin st

Long & Short st

Satin st

Satin st

Straight st, 2 times

Satin st

Long & Short st

Satin st

French Knot st   Satin st

Lazy Daisy st + Straight st

Outline st

80% Scale Pattern. Enlarge the 80% scale pattern to 125% to produce the full-size pattern.

Color #

Stitches and Color #:   Use two strands of floss. Use outline stitch for contours and elongated shapes. Use satin stitch to fill areas.

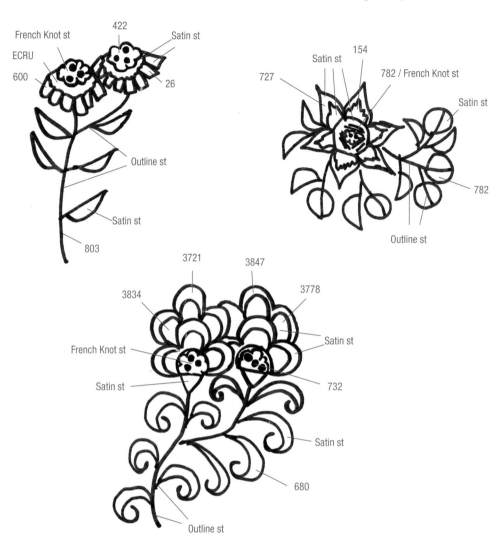

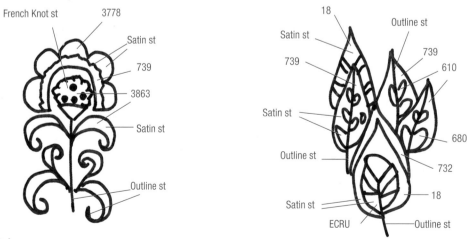

Stitches and Color #:   Use two strands of floss. Use outline stitch for contours and elongated shapes. Use satin stitch to fill areas.

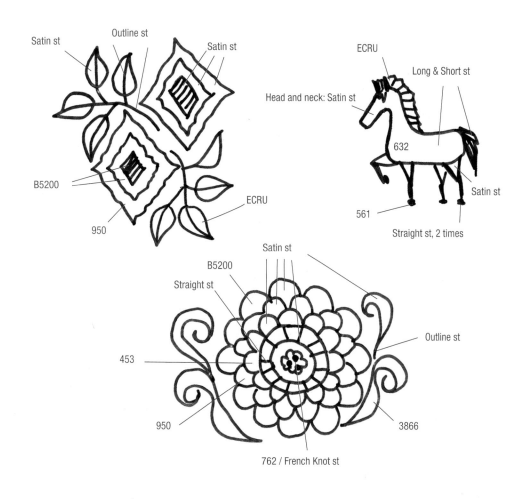

Satin st
Outline st
Satin st
B5200
950
ECRU

ECRU
Long & Short st
Head and neck: Satin st
632
561
Satin st
Straight st, 2 times

Satin st
B5200
Straight st
453
950
Outline st
3866
762 / French Knot st

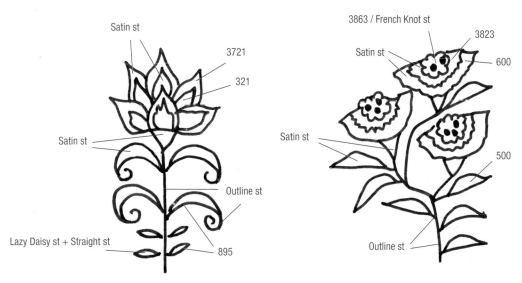

Satin st
3721
321
Satin st
Outline st
Lazy Daisy st + Straight st
895

3863 / French Knot st
3823
Satin st
600
Satin st
500
Outline st

p. 13 | 4 Bow Tie

Materials (Common)
Bow tie fabric (includes belt) 40 × 10 cm / 15¾" × 4"
Backing fabric 30 × 10 cm / 11¾" × 4" each
Brown: DMC No. 25 embroidery floss 333, 452, 550, 632, 666, 680, 700, 807, 3721
Green: DMC No. 25 embroidery floss 452
One 3 cm / 1⅛" wide brooch pin
Small round beads

Points
Embroider with one strand of floss. Outline pattern using outline stitch and fill in areas with straight stitch. Use the pattern on page 70; also see page 12.

Instructions
1 Embroider and attach beads on bow tie fabric.
2 Align bow tie fabric and backing fabric, right sides together. Sew along three sides. Then, turn right side out using unsewn side.
3 Make belt.
4 Butt ends of bow tie against each other and sew. Wrap belt at center of bow tie.
5 Attach brooch pin.

Finished Size:
4 × 10.5 cm / 1⅝" × 4⅛"

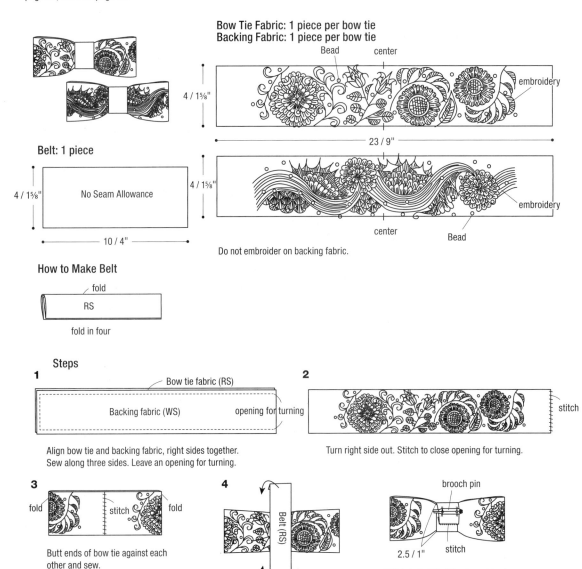

Bow Tie Fabric: 1 piece per bow tie
Backing Fabric: 1 piece per bow tie

Do not embroider on backing fabric.

Belt: 1 piece — No Seam Allowance — 4 / 1⅝" — 10 / 4"

How to Make Belt — fold — RS — fold in four

Steps

1 Align bow tie and backing fabric, right sides together. Sew along three sides. Leave an opening for turning.

2 Turn right side out. Stitch to close opening for turning.

3 Butt ends of bow tie against each other and sew.

4 Wrap belt at center of bow tie, and pinch bow tie fabric to create neat pleats at center.

Stitch to hold belt in place at back side. Sew on brooch pin slightly closer to top edge of bow tie. 2.5 / 1"

100

Top

Bottom

Use 452 for all stitches.

Outline st

452

3721

Straight st
550 / Outline st
550 / Straight st
550

Bead

Satin st

680

666

Satin st

550

700

Straight st

Outline st

Straight st

550

700 / Outline st

452
333
807

Straight st

632

Outline st

680
632
550

Outline st

Bead

Straight st

Outline st

Long lines: Outline st

▨ Materials (Common)
Fabric, leather 15 × 10 cm / 5⅞" × 4" each
0.6 / ¼", 0.3 / ⅛" wide ribbon 20 cm / 7⅞" long
Fish: DMC No. 25 embroidery floss 517, 807, 895, 917, 3041, 3722
Flower: DMC No. 25 embroidery floss 699, 895, 3801, 3860, ECRU
Small round beads
Seven pieces of 0.5 cm / ¼" diameter sequin

▨ Points
Embroider with one strand floss. Outline pattern using outline stitch and fill in areas with straight stitch. Use the pattern on pages 66, 76, also see pages 8, 18.

▨ Instructions
1 Embroider and attach beads and sequins on fabric.
2 Trim fabric around embroidered area and glue fabric on leather piece.
3 Trim leather piece to desired shape.
4 Thread ribbon.

▨ Finished Size:
Fish: 13 × 8 cm / 5⅛" ×3⅛",
Flower: 11.5 × 7.2 cm / 4½" × 2¾"

Fabric, Leather: 1 piece each

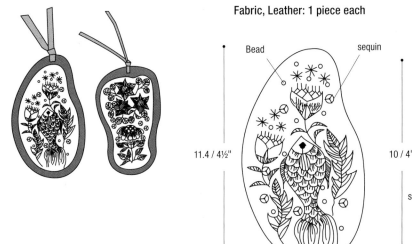
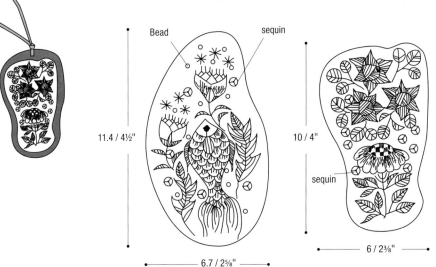

Bead · sequin
11.4 / 4½"
6.7 / 2⅝"
10 / 4"
sequin
6 / 2⅜"

Steps

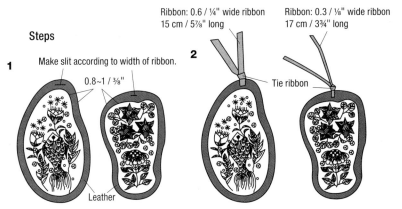

1 Make slit according to width of ribbon.
0.8~1 / ⅜"
Leather
Glue embroidered fabric on leather piece and trim leather as desired.

2 Ribbon: 0.6 / ¼" wide ribbon 15 cm / 5⅞" long
Ribbon: 0.3 / ⅛" wide ribbon 17 cm / 3¾" long
Tie ribbon
Thread ribbon through slit and tie off.

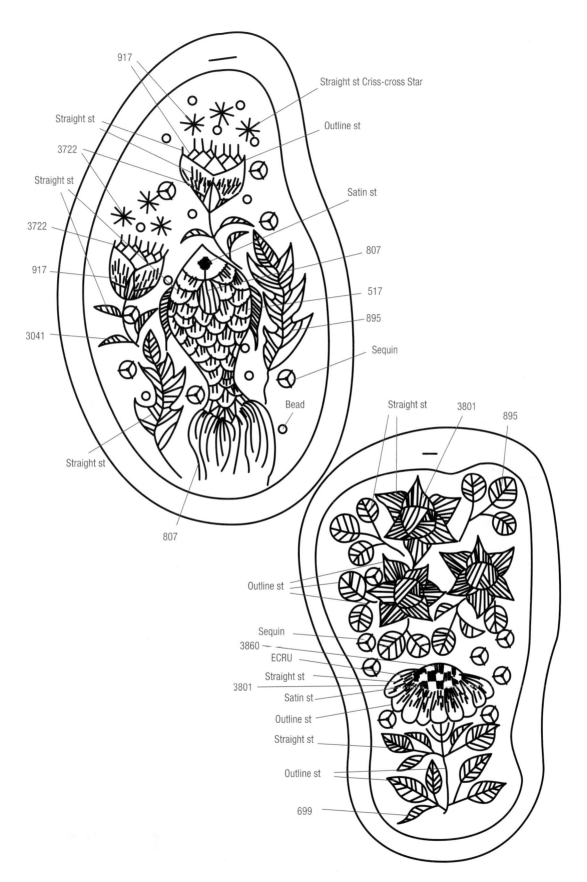

917

Straight st Criss-cross Star

Straight st

Outline st

3722

Straight st

Satin st

3722

807

917

517

895

3041

Sequin

Bead

Straight st

807

Straight st

3801

895

Outline st

Sequin

3860

ECRU

Straight st

3801

Satin st

Outline st

Straight st

Outline st

699

Materials
Band fabric, backing fabric: 10 × 135 cm / 4" × 53⅛" each
Delica beads (Japanese seed beads)
DMC No. 25 embroidery floss 310

Points
Embroider with two strands of floss. Use outline stitch for lines and fill in areas with satin stitch.
Use the pattern on page 82, also see page 30.

Instructions
1 Embroider and attach beads on band fabric.
2 Align band fabric and backing fabric, right sides together. Sew along three sides. Then, turn right side out. Stitch to close opening for turning.
3 Attach band on hat.

Finished Size:
Make hatband according to size of your chosen hat.

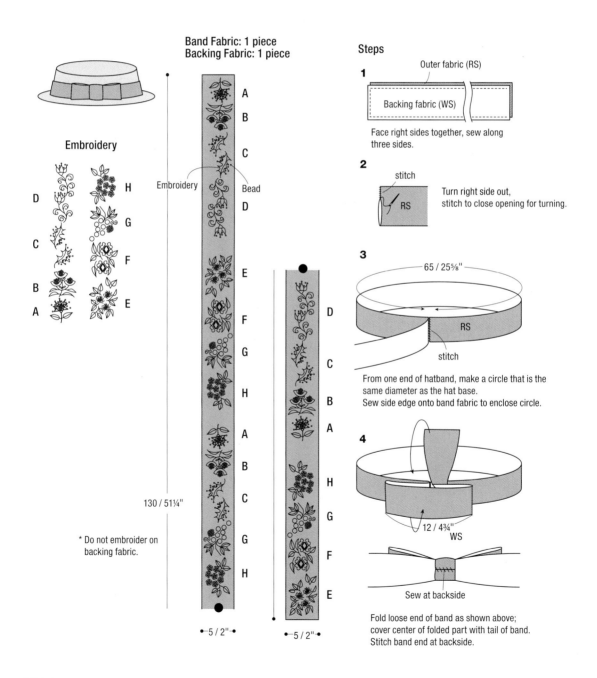

Band Fabric: 1 piece
Backing Fabric: 1 piece

Steps

Embroidery

A B C D E F G H

Embroidery   Bead

A B C D E F G H
A B C G G H E

130 / 51¼"

D C B A H G F E

* Do not embroider on backing fabric.

•–5 / 2"–•   •–5 / 2"–•

1 Outer fabric (RS)
Backing fabric (WS)
Face right sides together, sew along three sides.

2 stitch
RS
Turn right side out, stitch to close opening for turning.

3 65 / 25⅝"
RS
stitch
From one end of hatband, make a circle that is the same diameter as the hat base.
Sew side edge onto band fabric to enclose circle.

4 12 / 4¾"
WS
Sew at backside
Fold loose end of band as shown above; cover center of folded part with tail of band. Stitch band end at backside.

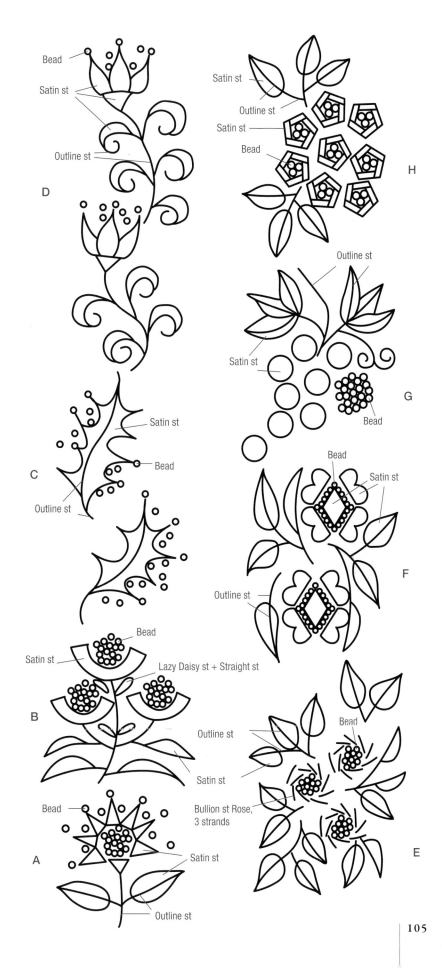

Bead
Satin st
Satin st
Outline st
D

Satin st
Outline st
Satin st
Bead
H

Outline st
Satin st
Bead
G

Satin st
Bead
Outline st
C

Bead
Satin st
F

Outline st

Bead
Satin st
Lazy Daisy st + Straight st
Satin st
B
Outline st
Satin st

Bead
Outline st
Bead
Satin st
A
Bullion st Rose, 3 strands
E

Materials

Outer fabric, lining fabric 30 × 30 cm / 11¾" × 11¾" each
0.3 cm / ⅛" diameter silk cord, 100 cm / 39⅜" long
0.5 cm / ¼" wide cord, 10 cm / 4" long
DMC No. 25 embroidery floss 310

Points

Embroider with two strands of floss. Use outline stitch for lines and fill in areas with satin stitch.
Use the pattern on page 83; also see page 32.

Instructions

1 Embroider on outer fabric.
2 Align outer and lining fabric, right sides together, and sew along bottom edge.
3 Fold along folding line and insert a loop between outer and lining fabric. Sew both sides and top edge.
4 Turn right side out and close opening for turning.
5 Thread silk cord through loop.

Finished Size:

9 × 24 cm / 3½" × 9½"

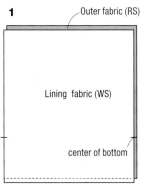

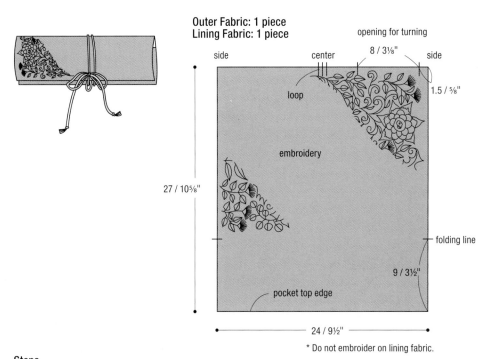

Outer Fabric: 1 piece
Lining Fabric: 1 piece

opening for turning

side   center   8 / 3⅛"   side

loop

1.5 / ⅝"

embroidery

27 / 10⅝"

folding line

9 / 3½"

pocket top edge

24 / 9½"

* Do not embroider on lining fabric.

Steps

1

Outer fabric (RS)

Lining fabric (WS)

center of bottom

Right side in, layer outer and lining fabric.
Sew along bottom edge.

2

loop

Outer fabric (RS)

opening for turning

Lining fabric (WS)

Pocket opening

fold   8 / 3⅛"

Fold outer and lining fabric, pulling sewn edge upward along folding line.
Temporarily secure loop.
Sew both sides and top edge while leaving opening for turning.

3

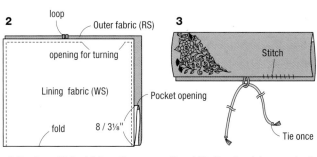

Stitch

Tie once

Turn right side out and close opening for turning.
Thread cord through loop.

p. 45 | ## 24 Drawstring Pouch

▨ Materials
Outer fabric, lining fabric 50 × 50 cm / 19¾" × 19¾" each
0.5 cm / ¼" diameter silk cord, 75 cm / 29½" long
One 1.8 cm / ¾" diameter cord stopper
DMC No. 25 embroidery floss 26, 154, 422, 600, 727, 782, 803, 3345, ECRU
Two types of small round beads

▨ Points
Use two strands of floss for all stitches except bullion stitch rose. Use three strands of floss for bullion stitch rose. Use outline stitch for lines and fill in areas with satin stitch. Use the pattern on page 90; also see page 44.

▨ Instructions
1 Embroider on outer fabric.
2 Lay outer fabric pieces together, right side in, and sew. Do the same for lining fabric. Leave opening for turning.
3 Fold seam allowance on unsewn portion of both sides. Do the same for lining.
4 Put outer fabric inside lining, right side in, and sew top edges. Turn right side out.
5 Fold top edges down and sew channel to thread cord.
6 Thread cord inside channel and attach cord lock.

▨ Finished Size:
35 × 19 cm / 13¾" × 7½"

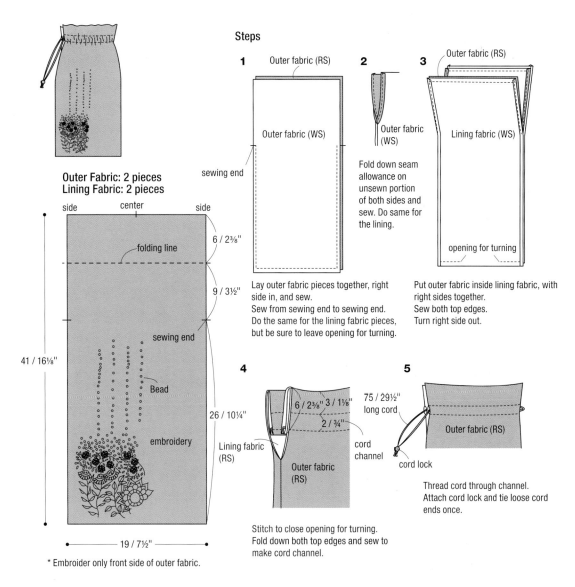

Outer Fabric: 2 pieces
Lining Fabric: 2 pieces

side   center   side
folding line
6 / 2⅜"
9 / 3½"
sewing end
Bead
41 / 16⅛"
26 / 10¼"
embroidery
Lining fabric (RS)
19 / 7½"
* Embroider only front side of outer fabric.

Steps

1
Outer fabric (RS)
Outer fabric (WS)
sewing end

Lay outer fabric pieces together, right side in, and sew.
Sew from sewing end to sewing end.
Do the same for the lining fabric pieces, but be sure to leave opening for turning.

2
Outer fabric (WS)

Fold down seam allowance on unsewn portion of both sides and sew. Do same for the lining.

3
Outer fabric (RS)
Lining fabric (WS)
opening for turning

Put outer fabric inside lining fabric, with right sides together.
Sew both top edges.
Turn right side out.

4
6 / 2⅜" 3 / 1⅛"
2 / ¾"
cord channel
Outer fabric (RS)

Stitch to close opening for turning.
Fold down both top edges and sew to make cord channel.

5
75 / 29½" long cord
Outer fabric (RS)
cord lock

Thread cord through channel.
Attach cord lock and tie loose cord ends once.

p. 41 | 21 Hairband

▦ Materials

Fabric (includes elastic cover, belt) 60 × 35 cm / 23⅝" × 13¾"
3 cm / 1⅛" wide elastic, 15 cm / 5⅞" long
DMC No. 25 embroidery floss 321, 333, 500, 550, 600, 700,
801, 895, 938, 3721, 3771, 3823, 3860, 3863, 3864

▦ Points

Embroider with two strands of floss. Use outline stitch for lines
and fill in areas with satin stitch.
Use the patterns on page 86; also see page 40.

▦ Instructions

1 Embroider on fabric.
2 Fold fabric in half widthwise and sew along long edge to make
  a tubular shape. Do the same for elastic cover.
3 Put elastic inside elastic cover.
4 Attach elastic portion to hairband piece. Match up edges and
  fold over extra fabric of hairband piece, and sew.
5 Make belt and wrap it around center of hairband piece.

▦ Finished Size:

10 × 30 cm / 4" × 11¾"

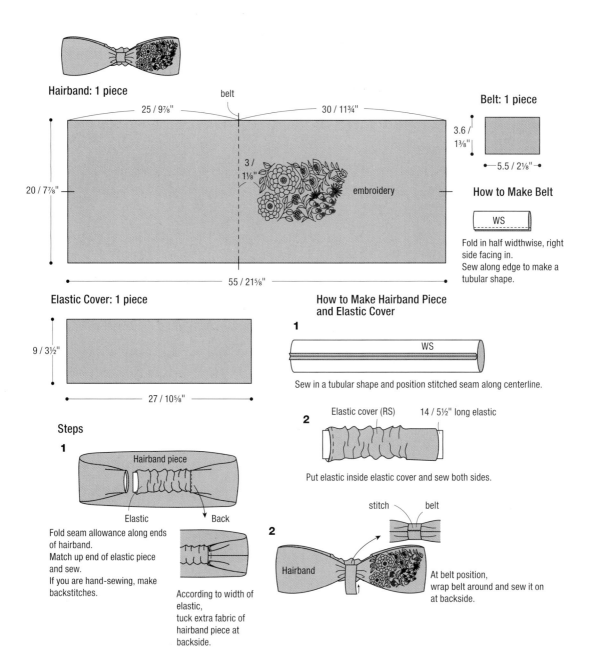

Hairband: 1 piece

belt

25 / 9⅞"   30 / 11¾"

20 / 7⅞"

3 / 1⅛"

embroidery

55 / 21⅝"

Belt: 1 piece

3.6 / 1⅜"

5.5 / 2⅛"

How to Make Belt

WS

Fold in half widthwise, right
side facing in.
Sew along edge to make a
tubular shape.

Elastic Cover: 1 piece

9 / 3½"

27 / 10⅝"

**How to Make Hairband Piece
and Elastic Cover**

1

WS

Sew in a tubular shape and position stitched seam along centerline.

2

Elastic cover (RS)   14 / 5½" long elastic

Put elastic inside elastic cover and sew both sides.

Steps

1

Hairband piece

Elastic   Back

Fold seam allowance along ends
of hairband.
Match up end of elastic piece
and sew.
If you are hand-sewing, make
backstitches.

According to width of
elastic,
tuck extra fabric of
hairband piece at
backside.

2

stitch   belt

Hairband

At belt position,
wrap belt around and sew it on
at backside.

108

333

Satin st

938 / French Knot st

3823

Outline st

500

321

Satin st

895

French Knot st

3864

Satin st

3721

Lazy Daisy st +
Straight st

Straight st

Outline st

Satin st

French Knot st

Lazy Daisy st +
Straight st

Satin st

700

3860

600

3863

French Knot st

Satin st

Outline st

550

333

3863

Satin st

Outline st

321

333

938

Lazy Daisy st +
Straight st

French Knot st

Satin st

801

Outline st

3771

109

Materials (Common)

Fabric 10 × 10 cm / 4" × 4"

Felt 20 × 10 cm / 7⅞" × 4"

0.5 cm / ¼" wide cord, 50 cm / 19¾" long

White, Green: DMC No. 25 embroidery floss 452, 775, 3024, B5200

Red: DMC No. 25 embroidery floss 680, 732, 3721, 3778, 3834, 3847

One 3 cm / 1⅛" wide brooch pin

Points

Use outline stitch for lines and fill in areas with satin stitch. Use two strands of floss to work French knot stitch. Use the patterns on pages 68, 98, also see pages 10, 52.

Instructions

1 Embroider on fabric and trim fabric along pattern shape.

2 Cut felt to same shape as fabric.

3 Attach brooch pin on felt.

4 Glue two pieces of felt on backside of fabric.

5 Attach cord along edge of brooch piece and tie a knot.

Finished Size:

Green: 11 × 8 cm / 4⅜" × 3⅛",

White: 8.5 × 7 cm / 3⅜" × 2¾",

Red: 11 × 8 cm / 4⅜" × 3⅛"

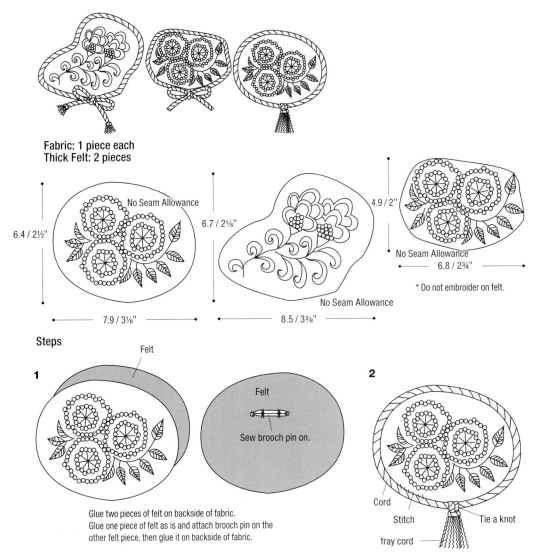

Fabric: 1 piece each
Thick Felt: 2 pieces

No Seam Allowance

6.4 / 2½"

7.9 / 3⅛"

6.7 / 2⅝"

No Seam Allowance

8.5 / 3⅜"

4.9 / 2"

No Seam Allowance

6.8 / 2¾"

* Do not embroider on felt.

Steps

Felt

1

Felt

Sew brooch pin on.

Glue two pieces of felt on backside of fabric.
Glue one piece of felt as is and attach brooch pin on the other felt piece, then glue it on backside of fabric.

2

Cord

Stitch

Tie a knot

fray cord

Lay cord along edge of brooch piece and sew it on fabric.

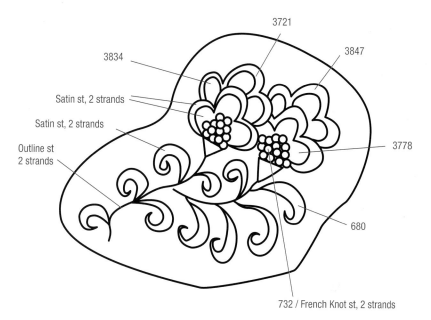

3721

3834

3847

Satin st, 2 strands

Satin st, 2 strands

Outline st
2 strands

3778

680

732 / French Knot st, 2 strands

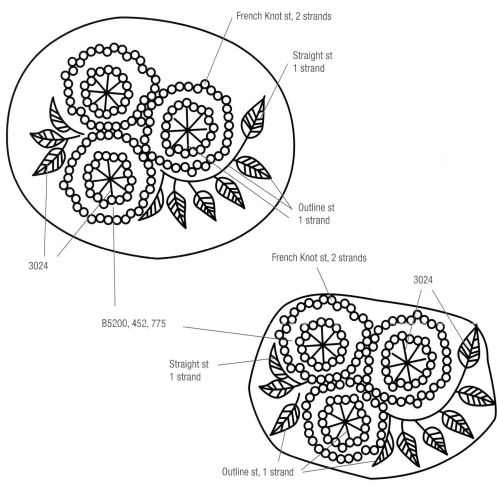

French Knot st, 2 strands

Straight st
1 strand

Outline st
1 strand

3024

B5200, 452, 775

French Knot st, 2 strands

3024

Straight st
1 strand

Outline st, 1 strand

About the Author

yanase rei

is an embroidery and jewelry artist. After graduating from Setsu Mode
Seminar, Yanase began making jewelry and creating embroidery designs.
She hasn't stopped since! Her work is widely exhibited, and her designs are
featured worldwide.

Originally published as *Shishu no Niwa*
© 2019 yanase rei
© 2019 GRAPHIC-SHA PUBLISHING CO., LTD.
First designed and published in Japan in 2019 by Graphic-sha Publishing Co, Ltd.
English edition published in 2023 by Schiffer Publishing, Ltd.
English translation rights arranged with Graphic-sha Publishing Co, Ltd. through Japan UNI Agency, Inc., Tokyo

Library of Congress Control Number: 2023931156

ISBN: 978-0-7643-6424-2

Printed in India

Published by Schiffer Publishing, Ltd.
4880 Lower Valley Road
Atglen, PA 19310
Phone: (610) 593-1777; Fax: (610) 593-2002
Email: Info@schifferbooks.com
Web: www.schifferbooks.com

For our complete selection of fine books on this and related subjects, please visit our website at www.schifferbooks.com. You may also write for a free catalog.

Schiffer Publishing's titles are available at special discounts for bulk purchases for sales promotions or premiums. Special editions, including personalized covers, corporate imprints, and excerpts, can be created in large quantities for special needs. For more information, contact the publisher.

We are always looking for people to write books on new and related subjects. If you have an idea for a book, please contact us at proposals@schifferbooks.com.

Original edition creative staff
Book design: Motoko Kitsukawa
Photos: Rika Wada (mobile,inc.)
Drawing: Miyuki Oshima
Editing: Ayako Enaka (Graphic-sha Publishing)

Cooperation: DMC, Atmosphere, Chappo, caikot

English edition creative staff
English translation: Kevin Wilson
English edition layout: Shinichi Ishioka
Foreign edition production and management: Takako Motoki (Graphic-sha Publishing)